THE

DAILY SPARK

180 easy-to-use lessons and class activities!

THE DAILY SPARK

Critical Thinking
Journal Writing
Poetry
Pre-Algebra
SAT: English Test Prep
Shakespeare
Spelling & Grammar
U.S. History
Vocabulary
Writing

THE *DAILY SPARK*

Writing

SPARK PUBLISHING

Written by Nathan Barber.

Spark Publishing
A Division of Barnes & Noble, Inc.
120 Fifth Avenue
New York, NY 10011
www.sparknotes.com

ISBN 978-1-4114-0228-7

Please submit changes or report errors to www.sparknotes.com/errors.

Printed and bound in the United States of America

20 19 18 17 16 15 14

Introduction

The *Daily Spark* series gives teachers an easy way to transform downtime into productive time. The 180 exercises—one for each day of the school year—will take students five to ten minutes to complete and can be used at the beginning of class, in the few moments before turning to a new subject, or at the end of class.

The exercises in this book may be photocopied and handed out to the class, projected as a transparency, or even read aloud. In addition to class time use, they can be assigned as homework exercises or extra credit problems.

The *Writing Daily Spark* gets students excited about writing by covering all kinds of genres, including hard news reports, essays, restaurant reviews, gossip columns, detective novels, and many more. While showing students that writing is fun, the *Writing Daily Spark* also teaches them the basics of strong writing, illustrating metaphor, thesis statements, allusions, and so on. It even covers grammatical errors, explaining how to avoid common mistakes like run-on sentences and misplaced modifiers.

Spark your students' interest with the *Writing Daily Spark*!

You’re the Sub

1 DAILY SPARK WRITING

Write a two-paragraph story about a day in class in the **first person** (using the pronoun “I”) from the point of view of the last substitute teacher you had.

An Embarrassing Topic?

Most formal **paragraphs** consist of at least four or five good sentences. Usually, the first sentence of such a paragraph is the **topic sentence**, which contains the paragraph's main idea. The rest of the sentences in the paragraph support the main idea. Practice writing a solid formal paragraph with a topic sentence and several supporting sentences. Write your paragraph on the topic "My Most Embarrassing Moment Ever."

Sweltering, Not Hot

Even the best writers rely on obvious words. Practice mental flexibility by writing a paragraph describing a typical August afternoon without using the words *hot, humid, heat,* or *sun.*

You're Not Supposed to Say That

When we're talking, we say *suppose to,* instead of the grammatically correct *supposed to*. But *suppose to* is a made-up phrase. To burn this rule into your brain, write four sentences that use *supposed to.*

Write one sentence about pit bulls, one sentence about politicians, one sentence about protractors, and one sentence about pears.

Belle and Sebastian vs. Creed

Write two paragraphs contrasting your favorite band or musician with your least favorite band or musician.

Mean as a Snake

Similes and **metaphors** are two ways of making comparisons. Similes compare things using the words *like* or *as* (*Angela is as sly as a fox*). Metaphors do not use *like* or *as*; they imply that one thing "is" another (*All the world's a stage*). Write a paragraph that contains three similes and two metaphors.

Poison Pamphlets

In the old days, feuding writers wrote **pamphlets** attacking each other's ideas. These pamphlets were inexpensive and quick to produce. The pamphlet form has been reborn in recent days with the advent of email and blogs.

Have you ever attacked someone's ideas online? Write about what happened. If you've never done that, write about the ideas you'd like to attack, and why.

Igloo Living

If you knew you were going to be banished to an igloo for the rest of your life, what five items would you take along? (Assume you would get all the food, water, heaters, and warm clothes you needed.) Write a paragraph about what you'd take, and why.

Last Valentine's Day, I Fell in the Bay

Think about your favorite holiday. Write down the first six words that come to mind, and then compose a six-line poem using one of those words in each line. For an extra challenge, rhyme line one with line two, line three with line four, and line five with line six.

The Giraffe Stands for Chris

An **allegory** is a device in which people and events stand for things outside the story. For instance, *Animal Farm,* by George Orwell, is an allegory in which the farm stands for the Soviet Union under Communist Party rule.

Think of a scandal or event that happened in your school, and write a brief allegory about what happened, making fictional characters stand for real people.

Beanie, Spiked, Slyly

Quick, name the eight **parts of speech**! If you need a little help, check out the list below:

noun: a person, place, thing, or idea (*aunt, cabinet, beanie, freedom*)
pronoun: replaces a noun (*he, she, him, we, they*)
adjective: describes a noun or pronoun (*pretty, dusty, spiked, orange*)
verb: an action word (*dash, whisper, skulk, frolic*)
adverb: describes or modifies a verb, an adjective, or another adverb (*quickly, grudgingly, slyly, completely*)
preposition: links nouns and pronouns to phrases (*in, on, under, around*)
conjunction: links lists, phrases, and clauses (*and, or, when, while*)
interjection: conveys emotion (*hey, wow, ouch, yeah*)

Write two sentences. Between the two of them, use every single part of speech.

No One Needs Email

A **thesis** is the main idea of a paper or essay; it must be something arguable. "*The Yellow Wallpaper* explores the role of women in society" is not a thesis, because no one could reasonably contradict it. "*The Yellow Wallpaper* blames the main character for her own madness" *is* a thesis, because someone could contradict it.

Write a thesis paragraph on the topic "The Importance of Email." The paragraph must make an arguable claim.

I Would Eat Ice Cream for Breakfast, Lunch, and Dinner

The **conditional** is the verb form we use to describe something uncertain, something that's conditional upon something else. You can memorize the conditional formula; it goes "If . . . were . . . would." Look at this sentence:

If I was queen, I would never have to study for a standardized test.

Was may sound right when you first read this sentence, but, when in doubt, remember the formula. *Was* violates the formula. The sentence should read, *If I were queen, I would never have to study for a standardized test.* Write five sentences that use the conditional correctly.

Inventing the New Checkers

New board games come out all the time, but very few of them catch on. Describe a new board game that you think could be a big hit.

When I Was Your Age . . .

Twenty years have passed, and your high school has invited you to be the keynote speaker at a graduation ceremony. Write a speech in which you give advice to the seniors and discuss what your own life has been like in the years since you've graduated.

Against the Capitol I Met a Lion

Foreshadowing is the technique of providing clues about what's to come in the story without actually giving away the plot. A writer might use a storm to foreshadow a death, or a bizarre occurrence in nature to foreshadow a political revolution.

Write a paragraph foreshadowing one of the following events: the inheritance of a fortune, the downfall of a major corporation, or the discovery of a crime.

Where's the Sequel?

What's your favorite commercial? Suppose you work in advertising, and you've been assigned to write a "sequel" to this commercial. Write a short summary of this new ad. If you have time, write a script for it too.

An Army of Everyone

Persuasive writing tries to convince readers of something. Skilled persuasive writers can be convincing about any position, even one they don't believe in themselves.

Try your hand at persuasive writing: Compose three paragraphs arguing that every American teenager should be required to serve in the army for two years.

After Soho House, It's Off to the Spa

If you could be any celebrity for one day, who would you be? Write a paragraph explaining why you would want to be this person. Write a second paragraph about what you'd do if you got to be this person for a day.

Slippery Syllables

Onomatopoeia refers to words that sound like their meaning. For instance, *fizz* sounds fizzy, and *languid* sounds lazy and relaxed. Try to come up with ten onomatopoeic words on your own.

I Hid During Snacktime

If you're tired of conveying emotion with sentences like *Randy was frightened* or *Sandy was happy*, try describing body language: *Randy cowered under his blanket* or *A grin lit up Sandy's face*, for example.

Write a story about your first day of kindergarten and express the emotions you felt by describing your body language.

Love, Valor, Freewriting

To **freewrite**, you must write *without stopping* for a designated period of time. While freewriting, don't pause to think of the perfect word or to get your thoughts in order. Don't even worry about spelling or punctuation. Just write whatever pops into your head.

Freewrite for five minutes on the topic of love.

The Importance of Being Witty

Oscar Wilde, one of the wittiest writers in the English language, is famous for his ability to write smart banter. A representative excerpt, from *The Importance of Being Earnest*:

LADY BRACKNELL: **Are your parents living?**
JACK: **I have lost both my parents.**
LADY BRACKNELL: **To lose one parent, Mr. Worthing, may be regarded as a misfortune; to lose both looks like carelessness.**

Try writing a Wildean dialogue between two people. Be as witty as possible.

Angry as an Undertipped Waitress

Some of the most effective **similes** and **metaphors** make unexpected comparisons. *Sly as a fox* is a bit of a cliché, so a reader's eyes might glaze over when she encounters it, but she would notice a simile like *sly as a hungry ferret.*

Write a paragraph that contains three clever, original comparisons.

Never Do Your Homework Ten Minutes Before Class

Suppose you've been hired to write a book called *The Secrets of Brilliant Students.* Write a sample paragraph from this book.

Marilyn Monroe and Tupac

If you could observe any two people from any time in history having a conversation, whom would you choose to observe? Create a dialogue between these two people in script form. The subject of the dialogue should be happiness and what people can do to achieve it. Each participant in the conversation should speak at least four times.

Bouncing Off the Wall, Betsy Caught the Ball

When **clauses** modify the wrong word, confusion results. Observe the following **misplaced modifier**: *Running down the stairs, the phone fell from Melissa's hand.* Melissa was probably the one running down the stairs, but according to the sentence, the phone was doing the running. The sentence should read: *Running down the stairs, Melissa dropped the phone.*

Rewrite the following sentences to eliminate the dangling and misplaced modifiers:

Falling out of his chair and onto the floor, the tailbone cracked.
As she jumped over the fence, my grandma looked up just in time to see the dog escaping from the yard.
Smelling like sweaty shoes, Estefan found the socks in his gym bag.

Then I Took a Pretzel and . . .

Imagine that you fell down a mine shaft with nothing more than a pair of extra socks, some dental floss, a miniflashlight, a bag of pretzels, and a set of keys. You managed to survive for two days and then freed yourself. In three to five paragraphs, tell the story of how you escaped. Try to create a suspenseful mood for your story.

For Breakfast, I Ate . . .

Many people enjoy keeping a journal. Writing in a journal is a good way of expressing yourself, and it's fun (and possibly embarrassing) to read over your journal when you're older. Write a brief journal entry about your day today. Be honest, and include mundane details.

Slurp, Crack, Lull

Ready for some more **onomatopoeia** action? Read the following sentences:

> **When Emily opened her soda, the sound was so loud that it woke her baby sister, who began to cry. Startled, Emily dropped her soda, which made a noise when it hit the floor.**

A few onomatopoeic words can spice up that boring paragraph. For example:

> **When Emily opened her soda, the *crack* was so loud that it woke her baby sister, who began to *screech*. Startled, Emily dropped her soda, which *burst* when it hit the floor.**

Now it's your turn. First, write five plain, nondescript sentences. Then make them more interesting by using onomatopoeic words.

Lip-Synching Hall of Fame

If you could create a hall of fame, what would you devote it to? Write a paragraph about what topic you think deserves a hall of fame. Then write two short biographies of your first two inductees.

For Example, Look at Donald Trump

Most successful high school **essays** consist of five paragraphs: an **introductory paragraph** (also called the **thesis paragraph**); three **supporting paragraphs**, each explaining a separate point; and a **concluding paragraph** that sums up your main claims.

Write your own five-paragraph essay in response to the following claim: *Rich people are happy.*

Shines Like the Sun

Imagine that you are the very poetic head of a cleaning crew. Create a list of the ten things the crew must do, using **similes** and **metaphors** to describe each item (*Clean the kitchen floor until it sparkles like diamonds,* for example).

Read My Lips: Free MP3s for Everyone!

A **stump speech** is a speech made over and over on the campaign trail. Typically, it covers the candidate's major policies and lays out a vision for the future. Write out the stump speech you'd make if you were running for office.

It Was the Best of Times, It Was the Worst of Times

The **first line of a story** often serves two purposes: to set the scene and to grab the reader's attention. A few classic first lines are burned into America's collective consciousness: "Long ago in a galaxy far, far away . . . ," "Call me Ishmael," and "Once upon a time . . ." are a few examples.

Create five new first lines of your own or, if you prefer, quote five other classic first lines.

Pause Here

Commas can be used to tell the reader to pause. For example:

> Thanks to his great attitude and impressive skills, Mike easily earned a place on the cheerleading squad.

Write four sentences that use commas in this way.

Donkey, Elephant, Neither?

Write two paragraphs about your views on American politics. Be open and honest; it's often easier to discuss politics in writing than it is in conversation.

Thailand, England, Australia?

Where would you most like to go on vacation? Imagine that money is no object. Write a few paragraphs about where you'd go, and why.

I'm Basically Positive

In your writing, strive for accuracy, but don't qualify every other assertion with words like *rather, mostly, little, extremely, really,* and so on. Rewrite the following paragraph, removing all **qualifiers**:

> Although almost everyone should be allowed to eat pretty much whatever he or she wants, I basically draw the line at eating pesto for breakfast. My little brother completely refuses to eat anything even slightly normal in the morning: he fully insists on eating pasta with pesto. My mother doesn't really care, but I usually get really annoyed by it.

"Then I Said, Like, What?"

Create a dialogue between the two ditziest people you can imagine, such as Bambi and Biff. Each character should speak at least ten times.

Amanda Destroyed His Tree House

Altering a word or two can completely change the meaning of a sentence. Rewrite the sentence below six times, each time changing two words. An example has been included for you.

Serge opened his birthday present.

Serge opened his cellar door.

A Lot of Parrot Paraphernalia

Believe it or not, the word *alot* does not exist. It is a made-up word that is never grammatically correct. Always use the phrase *a lot* instead. To ensure that you never, ever forget this rule, write four sentences using *a lot*. Write one about parrots, one about free speech, one about bicycles, and one about Freud.

Lottery Tickets Are Involved

Imagine you're a gas station attendant and are really bored at work. What do you do to amuse yourself? Write an account of your tactics.

Don't Trust Them

An **unreliable narrator**, as you might guess, is a narrator who can't be trusted. Many novels, including Ford Maddox Ford's *The Good Soldier* and F. Scott Fitzgerald's *The Great Gatsby,* are told in the first person by people who, as we eventually realize, mislead us or get the story wrong.

Write a few paragraphs in the **first person** (using the pronoun "I") of an unreliable narrator. By the end of your last paragraph, your readers should be able to tell that the narrator can't be trusted.

In My Humble Opinion, Your Facts Are Wrong

Fact refers to something that can be proven true, while **opinion** refers to something a person believes or perceives. Think about the last movie you saw. Write three factual sentences about the movie. Then write three sentences that describe your opinions about the movie. If you were writing about *Old School*, for example, two of your sentences might read:

Fact: Many people really loved the movie *Old School*.

Opinion: I consider *Old School* one of the stupidest, most offensive movies ever made.

Casablanca II

Come up with an idea for a sequel to one of your favorite movies. Write a 100-word **synopsis**, or summary, of the sequel.

Extra! Extra! Read All About It!

Write a news account of the latest controversy or event at your school. Adopt the tone of an alarmist, gossipy tabloid paper.

A Seat from Fenway, Elvis's Guitar

If you had all the money in the world and you could own any one piece of memorabilia, what would you choose? Answer this question by writing a paragraph that has a topic sentence and at least four supporting sentences.

If I Could Have Gone to Harvard . . .

Could've is the contraction of *could have.* People sometimes write *could of* when they mean *could've* or *could have.* Unfortunately, *could of* is an imaginary phrase. Never use it. To memorize this rule, write four sentences using *could have.* Write one about rhinestones, one about fake nails, one about college, and one about a suitcase.

Mac and Cheese, Chips and Salsa

In some newspapers and magazines, recipes are printed along with a little story that relates to the recipe. Write down the recipe for a dish you often make for yourself (even if it's just microwave popcorn), and then compose a brief story to go along with it.

The Writing Section Should Be Fun

The editor of the school newspaper has asked you to write an **editorial** (an article that expresses an opinion) about the new SAT. Write a three-paragraph editorial.

Always Use Transitions

Transitions are the sentences or words that aid readers in following the flow of your argument or point. Transitions can be used to:

show contrast: Katie eats popcorn after school. In contrast, Brian eats cereal.
elaborate: I love sneaking into movies. In addition, I try to steal candy while I'm there.
provide an example: You can get many useful items at that store. For example, Patrick recently picked up a lava lamp and a bobblehead doll.
show results: Manny ingested nothing but Red Bull and burgers every day for a month. As a result, he gained ten pounds.
show sequence: The police arrested Bob at the party. Soon after, Harvard rescinded Bob's acceptance, and eventually Bob drifted into a life of crime.

Come up with five sentences of your own, each one of which uses one of the kinds of transitions explained above.

Lobster, Caviar, Cheesecake

If you were choosing the menu for your last meal, what would it include? Write detailed descriptions of each item on the menu.

Fear and Unhappiness

In literature, **dystopias** are unhappy societies where people live in fear. The world described in George Orwell's *1984* is a classic dystopia.

Come up with a fictional dystopia of your own and write a few paragraphs describing it. What makes it so terrible? What are its inhabitants scared of? What is everyday life like?

The Mysterious Egg

Use the following sentences as the beginning of two different, very short stories:

> **Eve stared down at the egg in her hand. There was no other choice: she had to call F.B.I. headquarters.**

One of your short stories should be serious, and the other should be funny.

Algebra vs. Gym

In the context of writing, the word *compare* means "to discuss similarities between two or more things." *Contrast* means "to discuss differences between two or more things."

Write two paragraphs comparing and contrasting your two favorite classes. In the first paragraph, discuss the similarities between the classes; in the second, discuss the differences between them.

May I, Kind Sir, Interrupt?

Commas can be used to set off words that interrupt. For example:

> **Jane, on the other hand, has always wanted to try synchronized swimming.**

Write four sentences that use commas in this way.

Trucker Hats and Flip-Flops

Fashion critics attend fashion shows and write reports on them for newspapers and magazines. Choose one of the latest fashion trends at your school, and write a few paragraphs about it as if you are a fashion critic. Describe the trend, put it in context (how is it different from last year's trend?), and give your opinion about it.

59 DAILY SPARK WRITING

She Went Skydiving

Choose something interesting that has happened to you in the past year, and write a story about it. Write in the **third person** (using the pronoun "he" or "she"), and make yourself the main character of the story.

All About You

When applying for a job, you'll often have to send a **cover letter** that explains your strengths and qualifications. Writing these cover letters is difficult; you have to sound confident but not conceited. Perfect spelling and grammar are mandatory.

Write a three-paragraph cover letter to someone you'd like to work for. Summarize your experience and explain why you're perfect for the gig.

Introducing the New . . .

Write the script for a TV commercial advertising a new product that, according to you, the world simply can't do without.

Frantically, Hopefully

See how many **adverbs** (words like *rapidly, happily,* and *excitedly*) you can come up with to modify the verb *wrote* in the following sentence. Try to include twenty to twenty-five adverbs in your list.

Lucy ______ wrote her research paper in twenty minutes.

A Matter of Idiom

Certain rules of writing are just a matter of **idiom**—that is, they're only rules because of convention. Most uses of prepositions are matters of idiom. For example, we say, "I live on Oak Street," instead of, "I live in Oak Street."

Fill in the blanks below with the correct preposition:

1) He can't abide _____ the new Latin requirement.
2) I apologized _____ losing the hamsters in the heating vent.
3) I arrived _____ work three hours late.
4) He's in charge _____ making the reservation.
5) The puree consists _____ cream, egg, and garlic.
6) It's terrible to discriminate _____ parakeets.
7) It's impossible to object _____ her lucid arguments.
8) I succeeded _____ losing the hideous necklace.

Answers: 1) by, 2) for, 3) at, 4) of, 5) of, 6) against, 7) to, 8) in

Icy Hot Oxymorons

An **oxymoron** is the association of two contrary terms, such as *jumbo shrimp* or *same difference.* Write a paragraph in which you use as many oxymoronic expressions as possible.

From the Tip Jar to Your Pocket

Imagine you are a dollar bill. Using the **first person** (the pronoun "I"), describe what happens to you during the course of a week.

Kiddie Classics

You might think that the writers of children's books have a pretty easy gig, but good children's literature is hard to write. Come up with a plot for a children's book that is both appropriate and funny, and summarize it in one paragraph.

PB + J

Clarity is a hallmark of good writing. Test your own ability to be clear by writing, in paragraph form, instructions for making a peanut butter-and-jelly sandwich. To check the clarity of your writing, have a friend follow the instructions exactly and see how the sandwich turns out.

Fog Obscured the Old Mansion . . .

A story's **setting**—the location or locations in which it takes place—often determines the mood of the story. If the writer describes the setting well, it can make the story more believable and interesting. Where would you set a scary story? In a paragraph or two, describe the setting in detail.

DAILY SPARK WRITING

A Terrible Loss

Imagine that you've lost your most precious and prized possession. Write one paragraph about what the item was, and why it was special to you; a second paragraph about how you lost the item; and a third paragraph about how you felt when you realized the item was missing.

Diary of an Explorer

The journals of explorers can be really compelling reading. Imagine you're an explorer in the jungle or the Arctic or space, and write a journal entry about a particularly dramatic or dangerous day.

Dashing, Leaping, Grasping

Verbs are the backbone of sentences. Think about one of your favorite activities—shopping, eating junk food, reading, riding a unicycle—and make a list of all the verbs that relate to it. If drinking hot chocolate is your favorite activity, your list might include *sipping, mixing, stirring, heating, slurping, boiling, spilling,* and so on.

Semicolons Are Fun; It's True

Semicolons, which signal a big pause, can be used in place of a period or in place of a conjunction. Here's an example of how a semicolon can be used in place of a period, when two ideas are closely connected:

> Roddy was dying to write a novel; in fact, he was toying with the idea of quitting his job as an accountant and writing full time.

Here's an example of how semicolons can be used in place of conjunctions, such as *and, or, but,* and *because*:

> I don't know if I want to go to Jones Beach; I'm not really in the mood for sweaty masses of people.

Write four sentences, two using the semicolon as a period replacement and two using it as a conjunction replacement.

The Meat Is Mysterious

Write ten sentences about the food in your school cafeteria. Five of the sentences should be **factual** and five should express your **opinion**.

Dear Principal

Before email, **letters** were the most common means of written communication. People wrote letters to their loved ones, to newspaper editors, to members of Congress, to companies, to enemies, and so on. Letters are still a great way to communicate if you want to be particularly formal.

Write a letter to your principal (you don't actually have to send it) about a topic that concerns you. Begin by introducing yourself, then express your ideas, and conclude by thanking the principal for reading your letter.

Alliteration Annoys Alex

Alliteration is the repetition of sounds. For instance, *Tiny tots trampled all over the tentative tulips* is an alliterative sentence.

Write three sentences, each one of which is alliterative.

Barry Trotter

In literature, a **parody** is a text that makes fun of another book, usually by imitating the author's style to comic effect. A writer named Michael Gerber recently wrote a parody called *Barry Trotter and the Unauthorized Parody*. You can probably guess which book it satirizes.

Think of a book you've read recently and write a short parody of it. Try to imitate the author's style.

Mountain Tale

Write a very short story that ends with the sentence, *As he approached the top of the mountain, he raised his hands in victory.*

Bubba's Biggest Fan

Rewrite the following paragraph so that it simply states **facts** and does not include any **opinions**:

> Bubba's is, hands down, the best barbecue restaurant in the country. Anyone who tells you differently is just stupid. Their ribs are huge and juicy; their coleslaw is creamy; and most importantly, everyone on their waitstaff is stunningly beautiful. The absolute best thing about Bubba's is their incredible barbecue sauce. I think Bubba's mother came up with the recipe originally. It's so good that it could convert vegetarians to carnivores.

Serene, Scary, Suspenseful?

The **mood** of a story or passage is the general feeling it conveys. A story's mood might be tense in one passage and light in another. Use the sentence below as the first line of a story, and then create six different second sentences, each of which creates a different mood.

Pierre sat quietly and stared out the window.

Sit-Ups for Your Sentences

If your writing sometimes seems flabby or boring, **passive voice** might be the problem. Passive voice occurs when the subject receives the action:

The tests are usually graded a full month after the students take them.

The **active voice** occurs when the subject performs the action:

Mr. Wigglesworth usually grades the tests a full month after the students take them.

Rewrite the following sentences, changing the passive voice to the active voice:

The test was passed by the entire class.
Sydney's hair was dyed red by the stylist.
The car window was smashed by the baseball.

It's Always Darkest Before the Light

What is the **adage** you hate the most? *Every cloud has a silver lining; Stop and smell the roses; There are other fish in the sea; If at first you don't succeed, try, try again?*

Write a story in which someone cheerfully cites an adage and you let loose with your real feelings on the topic.

That Glorious Day

Write a paragraph about how you feel on the last day of school—but don't use the words *happy, excited, finally, end,* or *free.* Think of original ways to express your feelings.

Bingo Manual

Practice writing in a clear and concise manner by explaining the rules of your favorite game. You can choose a sport, such as baseball or football; a game, such as chess or checkers; or even a video game. To force yourself to be clear, write as if your reader is someone who's never even heard of the game.

Profiles in Accomplishment

Imagine that you've become a very accomplished adult, and a reporter has arrived at your house to interview you. As part of the profile, the reporter writes a long paragraph about your physical appearance. What does that paragraph say?

Upon Awakening, I Hurl the Covers to the Floor

Mock-heroic works are comical because they describe something mundane in grand, inflated language. One of the most famous mock-heroic works is the poem *The Rape of the Lock*, by Alexander Pope. In it, Pope describes the theft of a locket using the style of an **epic poem** (usually reserved for subjects like the fall of man or the clash of heroes).

Write a mock-heroic account of your usual morning routine by describing it in melodramatic, grandiose language.

For Sale: A Splendid Sweater

Choose something you're wearing right now and pretend you're about to put it up for auction on eBay. Write a few paragraphs singing its praises. Be careful about spelling and grammar—studies have shown that correctly spelled ads receive much higher bids on eBay than badly spelled ones.

Mixing It Up

To avoid boring your readers to death, you must vary your **sentence structure**. Look at the following unvaried sentences:

> Teddy glanced at his watch. He couldn't believe it. It was already two o'clock. He was late for his job interview. He wondered why he was so irresponsible. He realized he might cry.

Far better to mix things up a bit:

> When Teddy glanced at his watch, he couldn't believe what he saw: It was already two o'clock, which meant he was late for his job interview. Wondering why he was so irresponsible, Teddy realized he might cry.

Write a before-and-after paragraph in the model of the paragraphs above. First write a bunch of sentences with unvaried structure, and then make them more interesting by experimenting with structure.

The *And* Challenge

Write a three-paragraph story that doesn't use the word *and*.

Putting the *Long* in Long-Winded

A healthy desire to make paragraphs long and impressive-sounding can lead to writing simply to fill up space. Don't do it. It's really easy for teachers to spot sentences that sound okay but don't mean anything. One easy way to tighten up your writing: get rid of those little phrases that sound good but could be said in half the space, such as *in my own personal opinion*. As a brain-stretching exercise, write two paragraphs that are as long-winded and wordy as possible.

Storytime

Write a **bedtime story** for a small child. Try to make the story interesting, but also soothing.

Chocolate Milk and Croissants

If you had to spend two weeks alone on a remote island and could choose only one kind of food and one kind of drink to take along, what would you choose? Explain your rationale.

To Smoke or Not to Smoke

Your city council is considering a ban on smoking in your town's restaurants. The members of the council have asked for input from the public. Write a letter weighing in on the subject.

School Scandal

Gossip columnists collect the latest dirt on celebrities. Write a paragraph about the latest scandals in the headlines. Use the breathless, dishy tone of a gossip columnist.

Cause and Effect

Many stories, particularly thrillers, depend on **cause and effect**. Write a ten- or twelve-sentence story in which each event directly causes the next event. Start your story with this sentence: *The bike messenger swerved to avoid a barking dog, causing the pickup truck behind him to screech to a halt.*

That's an Understatement

Understatement is the downplaying of a situation. For instance, if you looked out the window, noticed that a flood had engulfed the town, and said, "It's a little damp out there," you'd be understating the situation.

Write a two-paragraph story that ends with an understatement.

Keeping It Parallel

Parallelism means making sure the different components of a sentence start, continue, and end in the same way. It's especially common to find errors of parallelism in sentences that list actions or items. For example, read this sentence:

> **I enjoy swimming in pools, lakes, and snorkeling in the ocean.**

You expect the writer to continue listing items like *pools* and *lakes*, but instead she throws an *-ing* word into the mix (*snorkeling*). Because the items in the list of actions are varied in form, a parallelism error has been committed.

Try writing three sentences that list things or actions; make sure to pay attention to parallelism.

Strange as It Seems

Is **truth** stranger than **fiction**? Think of an experience you've had that suggests that it is. Write a few paragraphs about this experience.

Bodice Ripper

One popular genre of literature is the **romance novel**. Most romance novels are full of melodrama and overstatement. Read the following excerpt from the romance novel *Outrageous* by Norah-Jean Perkin:

> It occurred to him that he'd like company for that swim he'd been planning. Alix's company. He cleared his throat. "Say, would you like to go for a swim? It's still warm and—"
>
> "No. No thank you." Alix stood up abruptly, almost knocking the lawn chair over. She stumbled and Matt automatically reached out to steady her.
>
> He stood up, too, his hands grasping her arms as he stopped her fall. He should have let her go then. But he didn't.

Using this excerpt as inspiration, write a few paragraphs that would fit into a romance novel.

Viewpoint Variations

Perspective has everything to do with how readers perceive a story. To experiment with perspective, think back to the last time you got in a lot of trouble. Tell the story of your misbehavior from your own viewpoint, being as convincing as possible. Then tell the story of your misbehavior from the viewpoint of the person who got mad at you. Again, be as convincing as possible.

Magic Mail

Suppose the invention of a magical mailbox has made it possible to deliver letters to any person or group of people at any time in human history. To whom would you write a letter? What would you say? What questions would you ask? Write the letter you'd like to send.

On the Topic of Pets

Write a paragraph on the topic "The Worst Pet Imaginable." Be sure your paragraph includes a topic sentence and four supporting sentences.

Your Character

The best writers are skilled at **character development**. They know how to create characters who seem like real people, not products of a writer's imagination. Some writers come up with detailed descriptions of their characters' childhoods, likes and dislikes, possessions, and romantic histories—even if most of these details never make it into the story.

Practice your own character development skills by creating a character you'd like to use in a novel or short story. Write a three-paragraph minibiography of your character. Include background, a physical description, and a few quirky details.

Period Dialogue

It may seem a little peculiar, but if you have something like *he said* or *she sighed* or *they yelled* after a piece of dialogue, you have to punctuate the dialogue with a comma, not a period. You can kind of see why this is the rule if you look at the following sentence: *"Get back here." he said.* When you hit that period after *"Get back here,"* you stop, and then you have to lurch back into action with *he said.* The correct formulation is: *"Get back here," he said.* Write four correctly punctuated sentences using dialogue followed by *he said* or *she said.*

Friends Talking

The best dialogue mimics how people actually talk. Write a dialogue between two of your friends, trying to capture their real speech patterns.

Name Acrostic

An **acrostic** is a poem or a group of lines in which the first letter of each line forms a word or name. For instance, the following is an acrostic about pizza:

Perfection on a plate
Infused with the heavenly scent of pepperoni
Zesty and cheesy
Zero nutritional value
Ah! Pizza.

Write an acrostic using your own name.

This Is the World

Suppose you've been commissioned to write a description of the world as you know it using only ten sentences. This description will be placed in a time capsule that will be opened 500 years from today. What would you write?

The Thin Tree, the Cool Car

When used in moderation, **adjectives** help a reader imagine the situation or thing being described. Fill in each blank below with an adjective to make the sentences more colorful and interesting:

The _____ tree fell close to the _____ car, startling the _____ lady.

Without pausing, the _____ cat jumped from the _____ tree, terrifying his ______ owner.

Twenty _____ children ran across the _____ playground, screaming _____ profanities.

The _____ weather made the _____ holiday seem like a _____ vacation in the _____ islands.

Dinner for Five

If you could invite four people (living or dead) to a dinner party, whom would you invite? Name your guests and write a few paragraphs about the topics you'd discuss at dinner.

I Growl When I'm Pleased

Lewis Carroll's *Alice in Wonderland* is full of conversations that are both logical and crazy. For instance:

"But I don't want to go among mad people," Alice remarked.

"Oh, you can't help that," said the Cat: "We're all mad here. I'm mad. You're mad."

"How do you know I'm mad?" said Alice.

"You must be," said the Cat, "or you wouldn't have come here."

Alice didn't think that proved it at all; however, she went on "And how do you know that you're mad?"

"To begin with," said the Cat, "a dog's not mad. You grant that?"

"I suppose so," said Alice.

"Well, then," the Cat went on, "you see, a dog growls when it's angry, and wags its tail when it's pleased. Now I growl when I'm pleased, and wag my tail when I'm angry. Therefore I'm mad."

"I call it purring, not growling," said Alice.

"Call it what you like," said the Cat. "Do you play croquet with the Queen to-day?"

Using this passage for inspiration, write your own logical/crazy dialogue between a girl or boy and an animal.

Mushy as a Banana

Writers use **similes** like *scratchy as a cat's tongue* to make comparisons between two objects or things. Using the following objects as the second half of ten similes. Try not to resort to clichés.

tree	glass
monkey	banana
rubber ball	cloud
pencil	ice
onion	planet

Person of the Year

The **tone** of a text conveys the narrator's attitude toward his subject. The narrator can take a sarcastic tone, or a reverential one, or an objective one, to name a few.

Suppose you're a speechwriter for a celebrity who has just been named "Person of the Year" by the nation's most famous magazine. Write two possible acceptance speeches for your client. Write one speech in a humble tone and one speech in an arrogant tone.

Cold As Ice

In your writing, it's crucial to avoid **clichés**—overused phrases like *sweeter than wine, the kiss of death,* and *as luck would have it.* They make your writing sound trite, dull, and unimaginative.

To draw your attention to the problem, write two paragraphs that include as many clichés as you can squeeze in.

With a Name Like Sally

What's in a name? Actually, quite a lot. Especially in works of fiction, names reflect social class and personality. Can you imagine a femme fatale named Sally or a kindly plumber named Basil?

Create three characters that could appear in a novel—but do not name them yet. Write a paragraph about each character, and then choose the perfect name for each.

The Big Top

List the first ten nouns you think of when you hear the word *circus*. Use those ten words in a paragraph explaining what a circus is. Imagine that your reader is someone who has never seen a circus before.

The Five Ws

Ever heard of the **five Ws**? They are *who, what, when, where,* and *why*. Nearly all successful newspaper articles cover the five Ws—they're a vital part of getting the story right.

Think of something interesting that happened recently in your town, and write a newspaper article about it. Be sure to cover the five Ws.

Your Own Antagonist

The **antagonist** of a story is the person who acts against the **protagonist**, the story's principal character. In the story of your life, who is your antagonist? Write a description of this person, and describe the way in which he or she acts against you.

Hair Horror

Write a two- or three-paragraph account of a disastrous visit to the salon or barber shop.

Next Generation Reality

Write a two- or three-paragraph letter to a cable TV channel explaining your idea for a new reality show. Include information about the location for the show, the title, the kinds of people you'd want to be on it, and the way it would differentiate itself from other reality programming. Make your pitch as market-savvy and commercial as possible.

She, He, Them

Pronouns take the place of nouns. They have their place in our language, but they don't do anything to make writing more exciting. Rewrite the following paragraph, replacing the pronouns (which are underlined) with nouns:

> He took it out of the box and gave it to her. She took it and then she gave that to him. He looked at it and then gave it back to her. She accepted it reluctantly and stared at them. They seemed surprised by it.

Supernew

You have been chosen to write the screenplay for a new action movie. Before getting started, you have to create a new superhero to be the main character in the movie. Write a few paragraphs about your superhero; give him or her a name, two or three special powers, a physical description, and a background.

Modern Tale

Retell one of your favorite fairy tales from childhood. Set it in the present day.

Its It's

Its and *it's* are often used interchangeably—but they are very different beasts. *Its* signals possession. *It's* is a contraction of *it is*.

It's easy to understand why people confuse the two words. The most common way to show possession is to add an apostrophe and an *s* (*Dorothy's braids, the tornado's wrath, Toto's bark*), which is perhaps the reason people frequently write *it's* when they should write *its*—they know they want to show possession, so they pick the word with the apostrophe and the *s*. To avoid making a mistake, when you see the word *it's*, check to make sure that if you substituted *it is* for the *it's*, the sentence would still make sense.

Write six sentences, three of which use *its* and three of which use *it's*.

123

DAILY SPARK WRITING

Parent Switch

In the novel *Freaky Friday*, by Mary Rodgers, a daughter and her mother switch bodies. Write a short narrative about the day you'd have if you changed places with one of your parents.

Ronald and Arnold

Using a topic sentence and four or five supporting sentences, write one persuasive paragraph answering the question, "Do actors make good politicians?"

In the Middle of Things

We say a story begins **in medias res** when it starts in the middle of the action. The term literally means "in the middle of things." John Milton's *Paradise Lost*, for example, starts with a depiction of Satan after his fall from heaven. Only later does Milton go back and tell the story of how Satan fell.

Start your own story in medias res. You don't have to go back and explain the whole story in this exercise, since you're only going to write a few paragraphs; just focus on jumping into the middle of the action.

Beautiful Anytown

You've been commissioned to lure tourists to your town or city by writing a travel brochure. Write a few paragraphs for inclusion in this brochure, making your town sound as thrilling and scenic as you can.

Walking Like a Dog

Imagine that you pulled an all-nighter. Now you're in first period and you can barely stay awake. Write a narrative in the **first person** (using the pronoun "I") about why you stayed up all night, how you feel now, and what you're doing to stay awake in class.

Lips So Parched

Little Women, by Louisa May Alcott, is a classic novel laced with **melodrama**—sentimental moments or events meant to provoke reader response. For instance, here is a melodramatic passage about a character's illness:

> Every one rejoiced but Beth. She lay in that heavy stupor, alike unconscious of hope and joy, doubt and danger. It was a piteous sight, the once rosy face so changed and vacant, the once busy hands so weak and wasted, the once smiling lips quite dumb, and the once pretty, well-kept hair scattered rough and tangled on the pillow. All day she lay so, only rousing now and then to mutter, "Water!" with lips so parched they could hardly shape the word.

Using this passage as a model, write a melodramatic passage about a character's illness or death.

Weekend Morning

Think about a typical Saturday and write down the first ten words that come to mind. As an exercise, write a paragraph or two describing a typical Saturday, but do not use any of the ten words you listed.

Encounter on the Fourth

Write a dialogue between a teenager and his or her strange relative. Set the dialogue at a family reunion on the Fourth of July. Bit by bit, reveal the troubled history that these two characters share.

Hollywood Summary

As you might know from writing book reports, summarizing is harder than it looks. Good **summaries** should cover the most important details while simultaneously striving to interest the reader.

Think of the best movie you've seen in the past few months, and summarize it in fewer than five sentences.

Food Critic

Restaurant critics, who write about food for a living, often get to eat at posh restaurants. Even if you haven't had a meal at Jean Georges recently, you can try your hand at food writing. Think of the last really good (or really bad) meal you had, and write a review of it.

Theater Critic

Write a newspaper article about a school play or movie you've seen recently. Be sure to cover the **five Ws**—*who*, *what*, *when*, *where*, and *why*.

Math Class Mind-Drift

Interior monologues are records of a character's unspoken thoughts. Reading an interior monologue might remind you of reading dialogue, except the character is speaking to himself or herself, not aloud or to another person.

Reflect on the kinds of thoughts that run through your mind when you're bored in class and let your imagination wander. Then write an interior monologue in your own voice, recording these thoughts.

The Handsome, Rude Man Violently Opened the Rusty, Squeaky Door

Adjectives (words like *adorable, squishy,* and *rude*) and **adverbs** (words like *sleazily, quickly,* and *impatiently*) should be used only in moderation. As an example of what *not* to do, add as many adverbs and adjectives as you possibly can to the following paragraph:

> The man opened the door and climbed into his car. As he drove along, he saw a woman walking with her friend. After hours of driving, the man arrived at his house. He got out of the car and saw a stranger.

With a Nervous Grin

Rewrite the following paragraph by changing the underlined **adjectives** and **adverbs** so that the new paragraph has an entirely different meaning.

> With a <u>confident</u> grin, Jeanie leaned up against the locker and smiled <u>sweetly</u> up at Brian. She was <u>supremely</u> confident that he would <u>instantly</u> agree to go to the dance with her. <u>Slyly</u> putting her hand on his arm, she said, in <u>melodious</u> tones, "Brian, do you have plans for the dance?" Brian <u>quickly</u> glanced down the hall. Jeanie was bewildered by the <u>nervous</u>, <u>hesitant</u> look in his eye. "Didn't you hear?" he said <u>quietly.</u> "You're not the most <u>popular</u> girl in school anymore. I can't go to the dance with you."

Twilight Zone

Imagine that you wake up one morning, walk outside your house, and find that everyone in the world has mysteriously vanished. Describe what you do next.

Wall Street, Y'all

Choose one of the following scenarios:

A cowboy spends a weekend in New York City for the first time.

A Wall Street broker spends a week on a cattle ranch for the first time.

Write a two-paragraph account of what happens from the point of view of the cowboy or the broker, whomever you've chosen. Use the kind of language typical of your character.

Before Using Commas

Commas can be used after introductory words or phrases. For example:

Before diving into the pool, Sam adjusted her goggles.

Write four sentences that use commas in this way.

Dear Subject

A work of nonfiction about a person's life is called a **biography**. A biography written by the subject himself or herself is called an **autobiography**. If you were to write a biography of anyone, whom would you choose? Write a letter to this person explaining why you'd like to write a biography of him or her.

You in Thirty Years

Imagine yourself as you might be thirty years from now. You've accomplished a great deal, or not much at all; you're married, or single; you've moved to New York City, or to Japan. Whatever you're up to, you've decided to write an autobiography. Begin at the beginning by writing a few paragraphs about your childhood.

I Sail Over the Bleachers

Write two paragraphs describing the following scene: Andy Pettite throws a nasty pitch, but Trot Nixon hits the ball out of the park, winning the game. Write the first paragraph in the **third person** (using the pronoun "he" or "she") from the perspective of a fan in the stands, and the second paragraph in the **first person** (using the pronoun "I") from the perspective of the baseball.

The Child Sings Horribly

List all the **adverbs** you can that could modify the word *sings* in the sentence, *The child sings* ______.

Do I Know You?

In literature, such as Joseph Conrad's *The Secret Sharer*, people sometimes have **doppelgangers**, or doubles. Some people think that doppelgangers exist outside of literature. Imagine that you've met your own doppelganger unexpectedly on the street. Write an account of the meeting.

Used to Separate

When two sentences are joined with *and, or, but, for,* or *not*, **commas** are often used to separate the two sentences:

> **Cherry wanted to see an action movie, but her boyfriend insisted on seeing the latest romantic comedy.**

Write four sentences that use commas in this way.

Ad Critic

Ad critics review television, radio, and print commercials, just as film critics review movies. Imagine you're an ad critic. Write a short review of the best commercial you've seen or heard recently and a short review of the worst one.

Star Wars Meets *Amelie*

When pitching a movie, writers and agents sometimes try to draw a vivid picture by saying things like "It's *Rocky* meets *Sleepless in Seattle*" or "It's *Casablanca* meets *Road Trip*." This way, the person they're pitching to gets an idea of plot, tone, and types of actors.

Write up a one-paragraph description of a movie you'd like to see, and then create a sentence to describe it, using the "It's _____ meets _____" structure.

Snowed Again Today

Imagine that you live in a place where it snows all the time and temperatures regularly approach thirty degrees below zero. Write a letter to a friend describing your daily life.

Fifty Words

A **run-on sentence** consists of two independent clauses joined together without punctuation. For instance, *We dashed across the field at top speed we didn't want the cops to catch us* is a run-on sentence.

An extremely long sentence is *not* necessarily a run-on sentence. What's the longest sentence you've ever written? Ten words? Twenty? Write the longest sentence you can without creating a run-on. Try to create a fifty-word sentence. Believe it or not, it can be done!

Fantastical Prose

Fantasy novels have been enjoying a renaissance recently. Read the following excerpt from the fantasy *New Spring*, by Robert Jordan:

> "An Aiel would have wakened you by slitting your throat or putting a spear through your heart, Basram," Lan said in a quiet voice. Men listened closer to calm tones than to the loudest shouts, so long as firmness and certainty accompanied the calm. "Maybe it would be better without the temptation of the tree so near." He refrained from adding that even if the Aiel did not kill him, the man risked frostbite standing in one place too long. Basram knew that. Winters were nearly as cold in Arad Doman as in the Borderlands.

Like other fantasy novels, this one uses made-up names and places; it also uses a lightly melodramatic tone. Using the passage above as a model, write a few paragraphs from your own fantasy novel.

Seething Silently

Write a short story about a confrontation that occurs in a grocery store. The confrontation should be entirely nonverbal; the combatants in your story should fight without speaking a word.

The Fragment Only You Can Correct

Sentence fragments have a subject but lack a correctly conjugated verb. Sentence fragments can be difficult to recognize, in part because they are so prevalent in advertising. *The platinum watch only millionaires can afford* is an example: *only millionaires can afford* is actually an adjectival phrase modifying the subject *watch*. A corrected version of this sentence might read, *The platinum watch only millionaires can afford is gaudy and overpriced.*

Come up with four of your own sentence fragments, and then correct them by turning them into complete sentences.

#1 Teacher

Write a letter to your school newspaper nominating your favorite teacher as "Teacher of the Year." Describe the teacher in detail, discuss how he or she runs class, and explain why this teacher deserves the award.

Noshing, Chatting, Sipping

Make a list of verbs that could be associated with the school cafeteria. Be creative and try to think of at least twenty verbs.

The Obits

Obituary writers often write up the obituaries of famous people *before* they die, so the obituaries can be published as soon as the famous person has passed away. Pick a famous person and write an obituary for him or her as if he or she has already died.

Prison Memoir

One of literature's classic novels, Vladimir Nabokov's *Lolita*, takes the form of a confessional written from jail. Imagine you've been jailed for some crime, and write the first three paragraphs of a memoir you plan to write from prison.

I Went to the Zoo

Writing can be narrated from several **perspectives**. You have the option of **first person** (*I looked at Helena and sneered*), **second person** (*As you know, dear reader, cats adore liverwurst*), or **third person** (*Brian and Steve agreed to meet at the dead of night in the broom closet*).

Practice writing in the first person by composing a three-paragraph story about your first visit to the zoo.

Lie or Lay?

Lie, lay—who can tell the difference? You can, if you memorize this:

> You *lie* down for a nap.
>
> You *lay* something down on the table.
>
> Yesterday, you *lay* down.

Write six sentences that use *lie* and *lay* correctly.

You're Invited

Suppose you're throwing the party of the year. Write the official invitation to this party, bragging about how lavish and expensive it will be. Detail what you'll serve to drink and eat, what kind of music you'll have, where the party will be, and so on.

Five Favorites

Write a first-person account of a meal that includes all five of your favorite foods. Use descriptive language to capture not only the way the foods taste but also the way you eat the meal.

Email Translation

In emails, grammar and punctuation rules are all but ignored, but formal letters are more traditional. "Translate" the following email into formal English:

> hey babe whazup. i'm sitting around doing nothing. just finished math homework. miss fishmans gonna be psyched. it's the first time i've done work for her class in like two weeks. anyway if u want to go to the movies later i think i'm going with bill rachel and missy. later.

The Personified Object

Personification is a technique in which human characteristics are attributed to an object or animal (*the blank page stared back at me; the flames danced in the wind; the chair groaned crankily*). Write five sentences, each containing one example of personification.

Sweepstakes Mishap

The sweepstakes prize guys ring your doorbell and yell, "Congratulations! You've just won a million dollars!" After a few minutes, they realize they've made a mistake: they're at the wrong house. Write a journal entry about what it felt like to win a million dollars and then have it snatched away.

But I'm Innocent!

Imagine that while on vacation in a foreign country, you've been arrested for a crime you did not commit. In the morning, you will appear in court, where you will have one chance to defend yourself. But you don't speak the language very well, and you're not sure what crime you are being charged with. Write a short speech in which you proclaim your innocence.

Music Critic

Some music critics are lucky enough to attend concerts for free and then write about them for the newspaper or magazine they work for.

Imagine that you're a music critic, and write a review of the last concert you saw. If you haven't been to a concert recently, write a review of a great (or terrible) album you've heard recently.

Dearly Departed

An **epitaph** is both the inscription carved on a gravestone and the short commemorative piece of writing about a deceased person. What you would want carved on your gravestone, and what you would want someone to say about you after your death? Write both kinds of epitaphs for yourself.

Set It Off

Commas can be used to set off words not crucial to a sentence's meaning. For example:

> The pizza, which had been left on the counter for six days, began to smell funny.

Write four sentences that use commas in this way.

The Joy of Floss

Most dentists' offices are decorated with posters singing the praises of toothbrushing and regular flossing. Imagine you're the person who writes the text for those posters, and write two paragraphs about the wonders of dental floss.

Pencil Says to Backpack

Choose any two inanimate objects that you can see right now. Imagine that both have distinct personalities. Create a dialogue between those two objects.

Pascal's Trip

Prepositions link nouns and pronouns to other words or phrases in a sentence. For example, in the sentence *Rover leaped over the table*, the preposition is *over*. Think of twenty prepositions that could complete the sentence *Pascal walked ______ the stream.*

Dear Editor

Has any issue concerning your town or state been bothering you lately? Write a letter to the editor of your local newspaper expressing your opinion on this issue. Try to be persuasive but not emotional.

The Mystery of You

Sir Arthur Conan Doyle's famous fictional creation, Sherlock Holmes, is able to detect a great deal about people just by looking at them. In this excerpt from *A Case of Identity*, Holmes explains his methods to Watson:

> "As you observe, this woman had plush upon her sleeves, which is a most useful material for showing traces. The double line a little above the wrist, where the typewritist presses against the table, was beautifully defined. The sewing-machine, of the hand type, leaves a similar mark, but only on the left arm, and on the side of it farthest from the thumb, instead of being right across the broadest part, as this was. I then glanced at her face, and, observing the dint of a pince-nez at either side of her nose, I ventured a remark upon short sight and typewriting, which seemed to surprise her."

Write a scene in which Holmes makes amazing deductions about you.

I Need a Vacation

The University of the Bahamas has named you one of three finalists for a full scholarship to its College of Vacation and Relaxation Sciences. The winner of the scholarship will be chosen by a review board that will read an essay from each of the three finalists. The essay must start with the sentence, *I deserve the scholarship because* . . . . Write this essay for the review board.

They're Confusing

Their, they're, and *there* are often used willy-nilly, as if they are interchangeable, but they are not.

Their is possessive:

They lost <u>their</u> hearts in Massachusetts.

They're is the contraction of "they are":

<u>They're</u> the ugliest couple in all of Boston.

There means "over yonder":

Look! <u>There</u> they go! The ugliest couple in Boston!

Write six sentences, two of which use *their,* two of which use *they're,* and two of which use *there.*

Dress Code Essay

Suppose your school has just adopted a dress code that is much stricter than the current dress code. Write a persuasive essay either supporting or opposing the new dress code. Support your assertions with facts, and take a calm, reasonable tone.

Showing Off

Allusions are references to other works or authors. (*As Shakespeare says, the man that hath no music in himself is fit for treason*, for example.) Allusions can be a great way to show off your knowledge. Write a paragraph in which you cram in as many allusions as possible to great authors and classics of literature.

177 DAILY SPARK WRITING

Soaring or Sneaking?

If you could either fly or be invisible, which would you choose? Write a few paragraphs about why you'd choose that ability, and what you'd do with it.

A Year in the Life

Write a journal entry about something exciting that happened to you this year. Remember that the best journal entries are detailed, descriptive, and honest.

The Moral of the Story

Write a three-paragraph story that could end with this sentence: *So the moral is, be careful what you wish for.*

The Writer in You

If you could be any kind of writer (news reporter, gossip columnist, obituary writer, novelist, children's book writer, speechwriter, advertising writer, op-ed columnist, etc.), what kind would you be? Describe the kind of life you'd like to lead as this kind of writer.